MANATEE

A First Book

*Drawings and Story
by Donna Corey*

*Photographs and Captions
by Joe Strykowski*

Published by
SUNDIVER PRODUCTIONS COMPANY
Crystal River, Florida

Published by:

SUNDIVER PRODUCTIONS COMPANY
P.O. Box 807
Crystal River, FL 34423-0807
(352)563-0318 / fax 563-0267

First Printing, 1990
Second Edition, 1992
Third Edition, 1997

Library of Congress
  Catalog Card Number: 96-70668

ISBN: 1-879488-08-6

Book Design
Bettie Johnson

Printed in the United States of America

MANATEE

(West Indian Manatee)
Aquatic Mammal
Endangered Species

Manatees are the most gentle of all earth's creatures.

When we observe them in their world, we see peaceful and curious animals.

Manatees have few natural enemies, yet they are close to extinction. Humans cause changes in the manatees' world that may injure and even kill them.

Manatees depend on us for their very survival.

Oh, good, you do
see us. We're not always easy
to see.
    We are manatees and we
spend our lives in warm water.
Some humans might think we're fish.
But we're not. Like you, we are
mammals.

4

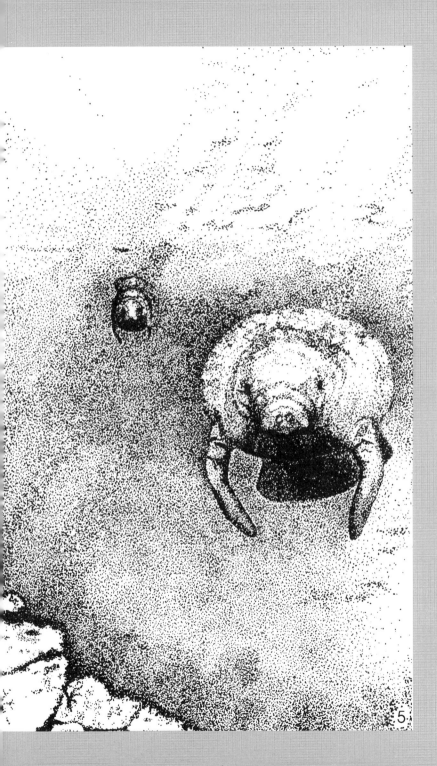

If you look carefully, you can see us just underwater. You can see our noses when we come to the surface to breathe. You can even hear us taking deep breaths.

Come in, the water is fine.
With mask, snorkel and
flippers, you can really get
to know us.

Meet my mother. Her name is "Piety." She is more than 12 feet long and eats lots of seaweed. She is often shy. I am hardly ever shy.

My name is "Bubba." I am one year old and already five feet long.

My mom and I "talk" underwater. When I hear her call, I swim right to her.

If there is danger, she herds me out of harm's way.

We manatees are very gentle. We don't bite or kick like other animals. We avoid danger by swimming away quickly. Manatees are lovers, not fighters.

13

I will stay close to my mom
for another year. She gives me
milk and teaches me which of
the sea plants are good to eat.
I nurse from nipples behind her
flippers.

We use our lips and our flippers to hold food and guide it to our mouths.

We eat so much sea grass every day that we help keep channels open for your boats.

17

Some manatees are solitary. Others--like me--can be very social.

My brother and his friends like to play follow-the-leader. When they stop, they might look for more playmates, for food to eat, or for a good, snuggly place underwater to take a nap.

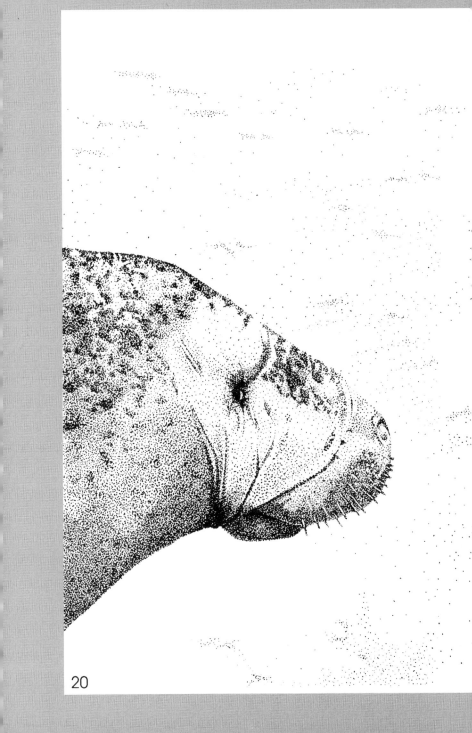

We are well-equipped to
live in the water. Our noses
shut tightly, and our ears are
so tiny you probably can't
even see them.

And we hold our breath a lot. Like you, we must surface to breathe.

Even while sleeping, we rise to the surface every 5 to 10 minutes to take a breath. When we're active, we breathe more often.

Pesky little fish eat the moss that grows on our backs. It's a shock when they sometimes nip us by mistake!

Our flippers are handy for swimming, touching, scratching, and holding things.

We have nails on our flippers that look like the toenails on our distant cousins, the elephants.

We use our flippers to "finwalk" across the river bottom.

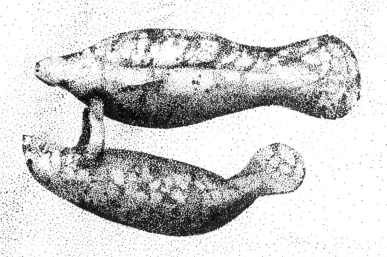

We steer with our flippers when we swim. To go faster, we just move our tails faster.

Manatees are curious and we like to touch. We touch objects we find in the water. We touch each other. Sometimes we even touch humans.

The ocean water gets colder
in Winter. To stay comfortable,
many of us swim into warm
rivers or the heated waters
flowing from power plants and
factories. In the Spring, most
of us swim back into the ocean.
    Boats are interesting.
Some of them have green moss

growing on their bottoms, and it's delicious to eat.

We try to avoid boats with running motors. They can hurt us badly.

Boaters can help, too. If they only slow down, we can almost always get out of their way.

We wonder about sounds we hear from the boats. To see us better, some humans get into the water.

We like to look at them!

We can trust humans who move quietly and slowly. And, you know, trust can lead to love!

28

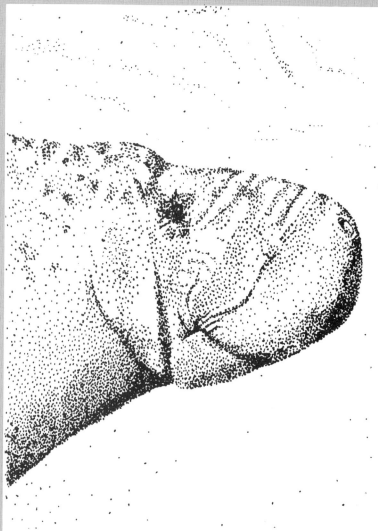

Maybe someday you will come into my warm-water neighborhood and we will meet.

That could really be fun!

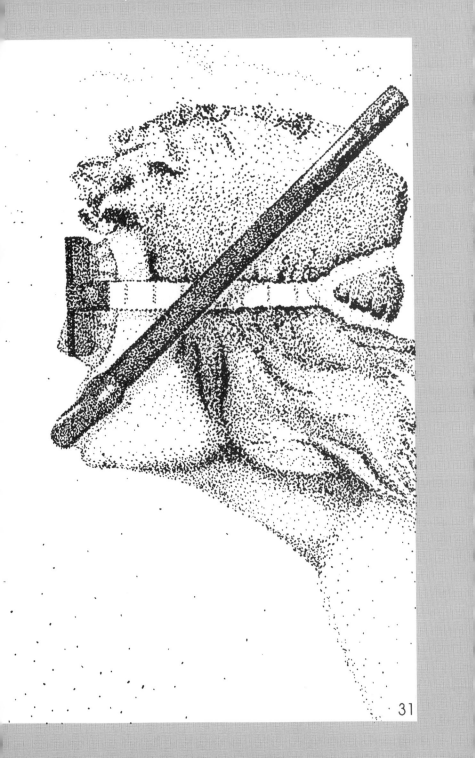

Manatees are curious. They often swim dangerously close to running boat motors. Boaters need to be extra careful when near them.

Natural resources officers discourage the touching of manatees. But many manatees enjoy human contact and often approach and touch a diver first.

Nose deep in a bed of freshwater grass, the manatee is an herbivore. Each day it can eat as much as 100 pounds of vegetation.

The manatee's nostrils close tightly underwater. But at the surface, they open briefly as the manatee takes a breath.

A young manatee chews my anchor line. A manatee may rub against an anchor line for the same reasons a cat rubs itself against a human's leg. It feels good!

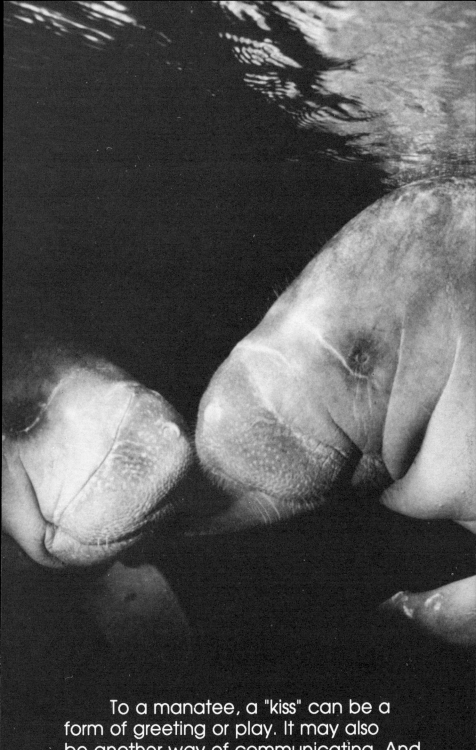

To a manatee, a "kiss" can be a form of greeting or play. It may also be another way of communicating. And manatee kiss a lot.

A newborn manatee may weigh as much as 75 pounds and measure 4 feet long. Here a baby is led to the surface by its mother for a breath of air.

The manatee is a mammal. It grows inside its mother's body before it is born. It is born alive and drinks milk from its mother's teat.

Manatees are playful. Here a lazy manatee rolls over on the bottom to scratch his back and take a quick nap.

The manatee uses its front flippers
for many purposes (to steer with, to crawl
across the bottom, to guide food into its
mouth and to scratch itself).

Manatees' intelligence and personalities are different than ours. But manatees are intelligent and do have distinct personalities.

Manatees are curious and often a manatee will grasp my anchor line with its flippers and chew on it. I call it manatee "flossing."

The manatee swims through the
water by pumping its paddle tail
up and down and steering with its
tail and flippers.

A diving veterinarian examines a cooperative female. The thumb-size teat is clearly visible under her flipper.

Manatees are wonderful divers. Most commonly hold their breath for about four minutes before surfacing to breathe.

If the manatee has taught me anything, it is this: if man could develop the manatee's patience, tolerance and selfless love, the world could be a far better place.

The manatee is in danger of becoming extinct. To become extinct means that the very last of the manatees has died, never more to return. Please help save the manatee.